THE FOREST OF LOVE

 A Love Story in Blank Verse

THE FOREST OF LOVE

TEXT AND ART BY
JACK PALANCE

A Love Story in Blank Verse

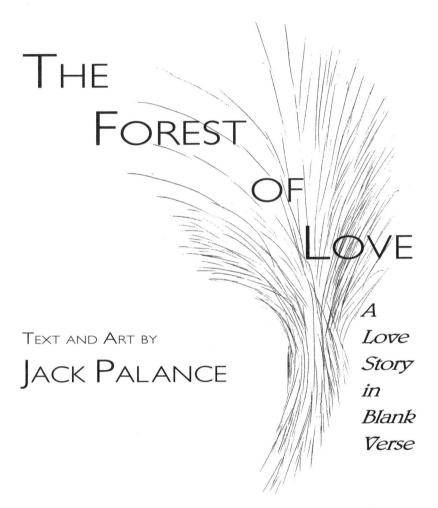

SUMMERHOUSE PRESS
COLUMBIA, SOUTH CAROLINA

TEXT AND ARTWORK BY JACK PALANCE
COPYRIGHT © BY CODY PRODUCTIONS, INC., 1996

Published in Columbia, South Carolina
by Summerhouse Press

Manufactured in the United States of America

FIRST EDITION

10 9 8 7 6 5 4 3 2

Library of Congress Cataloging-in-Publication Data

Palance, Jack, 1920-
        The forest of love / Jack Palance.
            p.   cm.
        ISBN 1-887714-07-3 (alk. paper)
        1. Love poetry, American.   I. Title.
        PS3566.A4559F6   1996
        811'.54--dc20   96-42025
                                            CIP

The Beginning . . .

The Forest of Love is everywhere,
And if love is a forest, love is a tree,
And a tree is Love.
There is nothing more beautiful than a tree, nothing
—Except perhaps the human mind.
This is where the tree is born, blossoms, is destroyed.
End of Love.
But with care and devotion
another tree will grow, another love will bloom.
Love has no numbers, no age.
It is infinite in its variety, in its breadth and depth,
in the coloration of its Indian summer gone mad.
The human mind!—
over which so few can exercise control
is the heart of Love.
Here lie scheming armies of exotic temptations.
Here lie brooding bands of angels and devils
poised and ready to soothe or ruffle,
embrace or repulse, love—or nothing!
And as always at the close, the forest whispers, *I love you.*

When I left you this morning
your lips were slumbering passion flowers
and I wanted to love you again.
But you were more than half asleep
and I was more than half desperately tired.
You were the most beautiful woman
I had ever seen,
and as I lay there looking at you
I reflected on the intense pleasures
now dormant in that slender love body.
Of course you know I love you.
I couldn't touch you this way if I didn't,
even if you are now, quite possibly, fast asleep.
I love you, but I don't know why.
I don't know why I love you.
Perhaps for the most primitive reason.
(How I envy those who can count the ways.)
I have only one way, then—
I love you because you are my woman,
—or were just a while ago.

Today you visited where I was working.

Last night we loved—today we were mute.

You were as lovely as you always are.

You were the woman I had possessed

so many times in the last weeks.

But now I could not reach you.

You, sitting there beside me, cool, aloof,

yet burning inside.

I could feel the fire blazing wild,

but you were gone and, strangely,

so was I, again.

How many times have we done this,

reached for each other and found nothing?

Is this all we have then,

a physical passion that consumes

and leaves nothing for in between?

I want to devour you,

make you part of me.

Then there would be no reaching, searching.

You would always be inside me and I in you.

How strange to watch you walk away,

not knowing if I would ever see you again.

Lack of communication.

I couldn't see your face—

What were you wearing?

Was it, it's over at last and thank God!

Or was there a moment of remorse,

I'll miss him.

Please do, if only for a little while.

You see, I didn't ask to grow old, or older,

before you were ready.

It just happened and then,

there you were.

I didn't ask for this, not now, not now.

I love you. And I'll run through the forest

to let them know. The Forest of Love.

But I've told you and watched your smile of denial.

Was that an arms length defense

or did you really not believe me?

Well, now you've gone, and I still love you.

Love isn't necessarily for always.

A week, a month, a year perhaps

and then moments of scattered remembrances

sprinkled like jewels

across the eternity of one's brief existence.

Love isn't necessarily for always,

but love is always,

and everywhere.

The sun, the moon, some lost tiny star

radiating hopefully across the pathways

of the solar giants.

Look for me, look at me, look!

I am love, I am love, please—look.

See the twinkling, blazing eyes of a universe

smoldering with an eruptive love passion

that threatens to derange a world of insatiable madnesses.

A week, a month, a year perhaps,

and then jewels across eternity. But love me,

and let me love you. For just a little while,

or for always!

The first time—
it didn't work, did it?
Dinner and wine, chianti wine,
and checkered table cloths.
You look so good in white.
But you know that, don't you?
It was white that first time and so I remember.
I remember looking at you, some far away madness.
But where? That I couldn't remember.
Burning, burning always, insanities.
And wild, feverish fires, out of control.
Alone somewhere, always alone, always burning.
On the cross, perhaps,
blood dripping slowly into little passion pools.
Sobs and madness.
Another place, and more. Darkness now.
Lost and found, out of control again.
Wait, please don't, please! Are you angry?
No, not angry. It's you! No, I'm not angry.
Then the fog lifted, and only your beauty remained.

Only your beauty remained.

And then flowers, red roses and white,

and little forget-me-nots.

Forget-me-nots, so soon?

Dinner again, and again.

Was it four o'clock that morning when he arrived—

he, your rejected suitor?

After how many persistent phone calls that you wouldn't answer.

"I don't know who and I don't want to know."

You were lying of course, but why?

Why torment him, what had he done?

Loved you, made love to you—

as I would do in a few days or nights.

Why is there pain in the ashes of love?

And why must love be punished, tell me why?

And then I'll ask you, don't please!

Not him or me—nor anyone.

My God! How many times have we inflicted hurt

and how many times felt the anguish returned?

Don't call anymore, please. Let me love what I remember.

Let me love what I remember,

now that everything else is gone,

and farewell!

It will hurt for a while, but at least it's direct.

Then very soon, no more calls, no more tears.

There are so many tears in the world today

that even they are in short supply.

Or do we allow the phone calls

because we fear that others may not call again?

And then someone is better than no one.

I love you, if—! Please, don't go.

I don't know yet, I'll call you soon.

Love, the simplest and most complicated emotion—

a bed of roses,

or a crown of thorns.

What color are your hemoglobins?

One man helplessly watching another fit his crown,

wondering of its adjustibility,

while the queen maneuvers to keep her growing love state

in a constant state of flux.

I walked out into early morning darkness

to find another traffic citation.

Fifteen dollars!

Small cost for what I had just witnessed,

for what I had just become part of.

I had earned the right to the explanations that had to follow

just as he deserved the right to those he was now getting.

The queen maneuvering to keep a king alive

with the help of a resolute pawn

whose only move was forward into oblivion.

How the pawn prayed for greater mobility.

How the king prayed to know his identity.

And where were all the other pieces?

When would they knock on the door demanding to be used,

demanding to be part of the game?

The board is small when the state is large

and the queen's noble mobility is greater

when the pawns are scattered

and her action sharply defined—

Protect one king and capture the other.

And the shuffling about in the closet,
how many more king's lie stifling there?

———

How many crowns have you collected, my love?
How many have you fitted?
How many who suckled your ample breast
are to your dungeon now committed?
And when they hear the phone ring, love,
do they quake in consternation
that the lover in bed must listen to
your soothing conversation?

———

It was George or Terry or Peter or Paul,
That's who I talked to out in the hall.

———

But no one cares who you talked to, love—
not in the beginning, anyway.

———

Then how quickly things begin to pale
when you've sat astride a mad, mad whale
who plunged to the bottom and zoomed to the sky
who hated the sun and spat in his eye
then came back down to his home in the sea crying
God, my God! Can I ever be free!

Where are we? I'm holding you again.

I lost you a while in the flare of my pen.

I've entered your valley at long, long last,

kings and telephones a thing of the past

—at least for now.

The whale plunged to the bottom then zoomed to the sky

while I, I, I,—how sorry am I, how sorry am I

for the whale, for the fish

who never got his wish.

He wished and he wished, but never got his wish.

That poor big whale, he's just another fish.

While, I, I, I, I plunged and I zoomed

and swam in the sky,

shook hands with the sun

who winked his great eye.

You've found her at last, you've found her at last!

Kings and telephones a thing of the past

—at least for now.

Out of seething madness that swirled me around

I foundered and sank then felt myself drown.

In you, my love, in you.

And when it was all over, the first time,

there was, as there would be many times,

the sense of emptiness, of not belonging.

Who are you, who are we?

We, the unlikely, the impossible lovers.

We'll meet again? Yes. When? Soon!

Then hours and days interminable.

If only the wind would blow or thunder crack.

If only the pine would rub across my bedroom window.

If only the pain would go away

and loving you would be again.

If only, If only, If only.

If only I could hear you again—

(murmuring faintly before the storm.)

If only there hadn't been that feeling of strangeness.

If only I could possess you again and not feel

that gnawing kinship with loneliness.

If only I would realize this was the first morning

and the years between would never be longer.

The years between, when will they be too many?

Will it be soon, or was it yesterday?

It's raining, my love, wild and then soft,

like you, like that musical giant.

I want to love you, today and tomorrow

and then for many tomorrows.

But not all, not all the tomorrows,

I can't ask for that much.

Do you think of the years as much as I?

Could all this have happened if I were younger,

If you were older?

And now the wind, the Jesus symphony.

But no one listens.

Oh, to the wind, yes, but I mean to him.

Tears. Trying to keep it all in order.

No, it would not have happened.

I am ready now for you, for your loveliness.

Yesterday the world was a storm—

today a symphony, you and I and He,

if he's real that is, otherwise, just you and me.

Almost every moment of my waking day

is filled with thoughts of you.

I don't know where this path is leading me,

but you're there, you're there and everywhere.

Madness maybe, for me at least.

Last night, again,

blazing insanity—

and not wanting to leave—no that's not true.

It's not being able to leave.

Then a hurricane whipping into orbit

with the centrifugal force of a hundred suns.

My God! Where is all this?

Sinking helplessly into the vortex of an awesome volcano,

I found myself erupted onto Elysian fields that do not exist,

in search of someone in whom I do not believe.

But this is more than just gratification, much more.

This is total communion, a spiritual oneness.

Many hours later, when it is all over,

you and I are alone.

He has gone.

Please, I don't want to lose you again,

You in whom I do not believe.

Stay with me and let me touch you sometime.

Or is that a sacrilege?

I saw your blood in the creek one day,

saw you bleeding.

I looked away for just one moment

and you were gone.

Am I finding you or are you discovering me?

If you are anywhere, I love you.

But why am I slowly going mad?

Is that where you are, in madness?

Is that where we shall meet—finally and completely,

the total one?

If I was sure you were going to be there

I would somehow hasten the process.

Meanwhile you've given me this woman.

What shall I do with her, will you tell me?

Is she one of yours, or an evanescence

waiting for me to become a meteor—again?

We were together once before, somewhere.

But where? You won't tell me—

and I can't remember.

Anyway, I know this is not our first meeting.

She's too deep inside me for that.

It's raining now and I'm alone.

Five o'clock in the morning and sleep won't come.

I lie here listening to rain and thunder

and then the wind rustling the leaves

which are beginning to color and fall.

Rain is so beautiful, a concerto of sounds.

Thunder is the cymbals and the base drum—

accentuating wind instruments, wild and driven,

then soft and lovely like your hands on my body.

Occasionally a lightning flash

and I feel you taking me deep inside again.

The trembling of your body—the gentle moan

are somewhere else, in some other world.

I feel myself moving through you and with you

and I'm frightened that someday this may end.

Walking away across an almost deserted parking lot.

Why couldn't I stop you?

Why couldn't I say something like, I love you,

I love you and I'll see you later or tomorrow

or somewhere?

You walk away and it could be anybody,

except the moment you disappear there is that terrible void:

my mind orders my stomach, my guts, to hurt.

Who is this mind force then, over which I have no control?

It does with me what it will, what you will.

As you walk away I feel my world dying.

Sounds—automobiles, people, planes and your footsteps

leaving me alone and mystified.

Who are you?

A woman, yes, I know, but who?

A spirit force that has entered my being,

that threatens to destroy or make me one again.

I don't know you, perhaps I never shall.

But then I don't know me, and never will.

Else I would have run after you. I love you, don't I?

That hurting deep inside is a strange phenomena.

Why down there, why not in the brain,

or in the heart which is the body's love cradle?

Why does thinking of you give pain and not joy?

How long will it last?

Is that why there is so much hurt

when love is so beautiful—

How long will it last?

I don't know where you are right now,

I wish you were with me.

Yet I can't call to ask you that;

though by now you've been mine many times.

I can't be free with you,

I can't forget the years.

I can't help thinking that it happened too late.

Too late. Where were you?

I searched for you, reached for you;

and found only occasional smiles.

You were on assignment elsewhere:

now you may be ready for me!

I have now decided to allow it
to take complete possession.
Madness!
On its own terms, in its own time.
Occasional excursions into its erratic patterns
have not frightened me—rather, am I intrigued.
Why are you doing this to me? Please don't.
No, not you, not you. Just . . . someone.
But in the ascension or discension into madness
when does one arrive, how is one to know?
Will there be someone waiting to take my hand
bidding me a profound or ludicrous welcome?
You have come home at last.
Will there be momentary glimmerings of this,
this world I leave?
I wonder if they have refrigeration and anisette,
daily headlines commemorating mass murder,
Exlax and Tylenol and natural vitamin E?
I washed the blood from your wounds and my creek turned red.
Will you be there to bathe my wound?

I had loved you, loved you well,

as you had loved me. And then—

Why? Two weeks, two long weeks of separation.

Where did you go, where was I?

A Grand Canyon on a postage stamp.

Sad, this. Do you remember me?

A chance meeting on a crowded street. Destiny's Children.

Your eyes, beautiful and warm—and frightened.

Why are you frightened?

"Shy," you tell me. "Shy, because of you."

Is it of me or the years that are mine?

Deep circles under your lovely eyes:

a tension that reached into mine.

Two long weeks of separation. Why?

Reaching out through the long, dark nights and days,

reaching for you. Evasive, elusive, at home,

waiting, waiting for the revelation.

Anxious, fearful, doubtful, suspicious.

Of what, of whom? You, or loneliness?

The well is deep, the walls are disappearing. Somewhere.

The spirit, or spirit force, where does it go?

In a bird, a fish, a man, a rat?

From whose bourne no traveler returns.

How did Hamlet know, or his creator?

How did they know the traveler had not already returned?

The spirit force, the life force, recycling, returning.

God! I know you, I have known you forever.

Where have you been forever, for two weeks?

The telephone . . . no answer.

A premonition of something evil!

The devil perhaps. Or nothing, no answer.

Why is that tree constantly at my window,

looking in to see . . . what?

The rubbing, the scraping, the murmuring of its leaves:

what are they saying, do they know me?

Does anyone of them know me?

A knocking at the door, no one there.

Let me finish, let me finish please! Jesus, please!

And the birds, their span is so short.

Could they live without trees, alone?

Can I live without you, alone? A tree?

Trees, the forest, have been a life-long fascination.
My earliest memories are not of people,
but of the apple, the maple, the elm, the pine,
and all of the others, all of them.
I stared at the bark of the white birch for hours
and sat in the willow counting its tears.
The poplar grew fast and had so many babies
I soon lost track of which belonged to whom.
When the wind blew I heard many cries in the forest,
cries of joy, and many of pain, when a twig, a branch,
or the tree itself snapped because of the wind force.
One day the tallest apple tree jack-knifed
and fell to the ground. A lightening bolt.
The large red apples rolled down the hill,
into a deep strip mine.
They cut the tree down the next day and I sobbed.
"You can save it," I said, "You can save it. Please try!"
No one listened and I ran into the forest.
"It died," I said. "The tree died."
I heard the forest weeping.

"Please love me," I said, "Please, I want to be one of you."
The forest embraced me and a blue spruce said, "Welcome!"
Then as the years raced by I ran through the forest,
climbed into its trees and felt the warmth
of its love about me always.
I was the forest and it was I.
And when the grass grew tall, I was the cowboy
who watched an almost naked Indian walking about
in deep, deep mediation. Quietly weeping.
Large tears rolled down his sunken cheeks
onto the wild flowers that joyously reached up to him.
He never saw me, never noted that my finger was cocked.
Except one time, only once, when he looked right at me
and smiled through his tears.
I wondered about the blood on his forehead,
but I was too frightened to ask.
Then one day, I went far away from the forest
and more than a dozen years were gone
before I returned, but by now I had forgotten,
I had forgotten the Indian, the wild flowers, and giant tears.

Why did you stay away from me for two weeks, why?

I wanted you so, I wanted you, but you weren't there.

Through long, sleepless nights I thought of the cross,

the blood and racing cowboys and Indians.

Then he came back to me and I went to him.

What was I searching for, what did I want?

Was it you or was it something far away?

That night we loved again and you were my life.

Have I told you what it was like, loving you?

Will you listen, please, please, listen!

My God! I am going mad.

And suddenly the night was gone, but this time I didn't leave.

I stayed and you stayed and he listened.

Loving you has become my religion.

Lying on you, spread wide open, is my cross.

My body, my strength, my blood enter into you.

Then finally my mind, vanishing into the recesses of your love,

holding me, feeding me, drowning me.

The explosion! And I am born again.

In your love agony my seed is my own birthing.

A long moment of love, a brief encounter with eternity.

And we talked,—was it the first time?

I love you . . . and I love you, too.

The first time.

Hasty qualifications, half truths, fear of nakedness:

who will throw the first stone and why?

Hesitations, explanations, reservations, trepidations.

But nothing we could say would change this night of love,

Nothing.

Not even the sun, warm, friendly, and curious,

lying between us and on us, romping about on ceiling and walls.

The two week famine was over.

When would another begin?

Not that day or night, nor the following day.

Then the visit.

Did you know I died when you walked away?

I died.

My world was a shattering holocaust of unravelling dreams

and I was back in the cradle of my spirituality,

back in my Forest of Love!

Always, have I loved walking through tall trees

hunting mushrooms: red tops, pinkies, kozars.

The sure edibles. The others were left to rot,

and waste their sweetness on forest pathways.

The forest, murmuring, weeping, sobbing, laughing.

The Forest of Love.

Lying amongst the trees and listening—

a stillness so acute lovers forget to breathe.

Will I find you there? Please come.

I want to build a cabin, over there—

on that little island that divides the creek in two.

The trees grow fast and tall and the water,

rushing merrily all around, sings the melody of forest love.

The stillness is broken and lovers breathe again,

whispering loving incantations:

I shall love you forever or till the forest goes away.

The forest smiles whimsically: It is forever.

And so are we, you and I. You and I and he.

He is here always. Listen! Did you hear?

Yes, that was he. Let me take you to him.

I died when you walked away
knowing I would never see you again.
The tall ugly buildings were gone
and Taras rode the steppes in search of a vanishing dream.
Freedom. He was never to find it, but he never lost the dream.
All about me the flora grew quickly, so quickly,
and a young doe ate fallen fruit.
Somewhere a distant voice, we need you. Please come.
Somewhere a body moving, gently moving—
touching, searching, entering. Entering a forest of love.
We need you, please come. Faces!
Faces with mouths wide open: screaming, laughing, calling.
Insanity all about me — the rope, the gun, which?
Ten thousand starlings moving toward the rookery,
moving thru the darkness that shelters their home.
Darkness, hiding the ugliness of a deafening city,
awaiting impatiently the next coming, the ultimate tremble.
Now I lay me down, down, down.
A city recycled, its spirit force clamoring:
I want to be beautiful. Give me trees, many, many trees.

Why do we stay, what are we waiting for?

It will never change, it will never be better.

The years are the alternative and we the alternative's children.

Trapped in an absurdity that races toward the inevitable

we swagger about in the empty convulsions of self esteem

waiting for the curtain to rise or fall. Was Hamlet right?

Was I right in letting you walk away with my life?

How much longer would I have had?

Might I have become one of your closet kings

waiting for a little man to pound on your door?

What did he think of me as his immediate successor,

and who was his just as immediate predecessor.

Was it he who stripped you naked on a lonely street

demanding to love you on a stranger's lawn?

Where did you go to regroup, to become the lady again?

Where, my love, where? Where are you?

Lonely streets are all the same and so are naked lives.

Something there is that dictates our behavior

and loneliness is the solitary pathway to the lengthening cross.

Watching its shadow come racing toward me, I heard the phone ring.

It was you. How are you, and other amenities.

I've missed you and I've missed you. Strangers. Far away.

Rising from the dead I could not rejoice.

Why did you call? It was all over.

You know I love you, dying can't change that.

Nor can living again. Can you hear the rain?

Reaching out once more is difficult, will you be there?

Will I know who you are?

How much have you changed in these three years—

or was it only three days?

A steady, rhythmic patter on the tin roof,

down to the gutter pipe, and into the overflowing rain barrel.

The forest is happy, that love affair is constant.

Will they remember me, will I remember you?

Something has changed, what? An emptiness now.

Wanting to embrace you, will I find you?

Will you come into the forest with me, will you?

Will you walk with me in the water of my creek

and love me on my island where music is forever.

I rose from the dead to love you one more time. . .

Standing on the brink of another dimension,

I tumbled back into the vanishing dream of El Dorado.

Through that long brief night

we loved and were one again

joined together once more

by that same gentle omniscience.

He must have known something was about to happen.

Why did he want this one more reunion?

"Are you kidding? I love loving you."

A rudderless plane spinning helplessly out of control,

approaching the earth at blinding speed

and then suddenly back at twenty thousand feet,

snaprolling, looping—and I love you.

Like jumping without a parachute.

My God! Those last seconds—

the agonizing beauty of the arrival, where was I?

The awakening, then and now.

Faraway and here. I love you.

But the forest, the flaming, whispering, screaming forest.

Will you understand when it happens?

I drove directly to the airport when I left you,

and two hours later

was on my way back to the forest.

Three thousand miles would be between us,

three thousand miles, a jack-knifed apple tree,

and a man who smiled through giant tears.

The stewardess seemed alarmed. Is anything wrong?

A cold, I said, just a cold. My tears were almost as large as his.

I was going home forever.

But you know I love you, don't you?

At thirty thousand feet I wish I could see a tree.

Clouds, enormous clouds rolling everywhere.

Is it raining in the forest? How high is the creek?

How many martinis can one man consume?

How much sleep have I had in the last three weeks,

how many bottles of warm white wine?

How old are you, you never would tell me?

Why are you sometimes sixteen, or twelve or forty?

But now the plane has started down and very soon

I shall be in the forest again, back in the forest of love!

I have never felt as strange as I do tonight,

running through the forest. Something is wrong,

but no one will tell me what it is.

A waiting perhaps, a waiting for something to happen.

Something ominous, but what?

The creek is lower than ever before:

the grass, the moss, the earth beneath my feet

have never been this dry.

All are happy to see me, I can sense this.

They reach for me as they often have before,

but the touching is more tenuous, more restrained.

They are waiting for something to happen.

"What is it," I whispered, looking about and up and down.

"What is going on? Tell me please."

The wind blew and the leaves rustled, "Shhhh....!"

I wish you were with me: I feel so all alone.

Please wait for me—I mean, oh, God!

I won't be there for dinner tonight, I forgot to tell you.

The wind is growing stronger and they won't talk to me.

Why? Please, Please don't ignore me. Please!

Walking slowly away from the edge of the forest.
I felt myself surrounded by an aura of consoling affection,
the grass, the earth, the barn, the Pennsylvania farmhouse.
Inside the house the telephone rang. How could they know?
I had told no one. I thought it might be the forest—
calling to apologize, or at least to explain.
It was you. How could you know, I had never told you?
"I know," you said, "because I love you."
"You make me happy," I said, "especially tonight!"
"What does that mean," you asked, "why especially tonight?"
"And why did you leave? You were coming to dinner, remember?"
"I remember," I said, "but something strange is happening here.
Something is wrong with the forest."
"What forest?" you asked. "What are you talking about? Tell me."
"I can't," I said, "I can't tell you. Not yet."
"Shall I come there," you asked. "Shall I come tomorrow?"
"No, don't," I said. "Not yet. I'll call you."
"Please do," you said. "Please."
"Goodnight, I love you." "And I love you."
The second time—and the last.

You were my summer of long ago, early and late.

I shall never forget you.

How can I? So few summers remain for me. Summers?

But now the crop is harvested, the beans are out of the pod

and soon the Pennsylvania earth will lie fallow

under a blanket of soft, thick snow

that will make it ready for the spring that must inevitably follow.

Tomorrow.

Then the love story begins again.

Prepare the land carefully, slowly;

make her fertile with seed that will germinate

and grow tall and green and make her farmer-lover very happy.

And the land will be happy, too.

From her rich, black loins will issue the abundance

of a fruit to be savored, suckled, then devoured.

How fortunate are we here, that the pill has not been discovered.

I have loved thee well, adored thee even,

but now the fruit has fallen and snow is drifting down.

Wasn't it a white dress you wore that first time?

Yes, I remember. I remember it well. As well as I have loved thee.

Was awakened this morning by the sound of starlings,

thousands of them in and around the rookery near my home.

Ten o'clock. Dear Lord! The storm is over.

Nine full hours of unbroken sleep.

The pain is gone, the burning has stopped.

Why was I burning, from whence the pain?

I thought of running into the forest,

but then remembered yesterday and decided to wait—

wait until later today, or maybe until tomorrow.

There was something very strange about my reception.

Was it just that they weren't expecting me,

or had I fallen into disfavor because of my long absence?

I intended to ask for sufficient reason, but right now

I wanted to wander through the barn and around the lake

remembering the loveliness of life and living.

Then I remembered you again and the valley was saddened:

it thought you would be here with me.

I think you would love it, I think . . .Something is wrong!

Again I wanted to run into the forest,

then once more decided to wait. Perhaps it would call for me.

Later, after a lunch of canned tunafish and beans,

I climbed into a large, black walnut tree

and studied the land that surrounded me.

Through my Zeiss binoculars I could see everything.

The kidney beans had been shucked

the fields were turning brown, deep brown.

In the forest I could see the colors

of a hundred rainbows waiting

for a high wind to blow an end to Indian summer.

The forest is so beautiful!

My daddy used to say that all the leaves

were hand painted by God and his angels.

I believed this at first, but then one day

I tried to count the leaves of a small elm tree,

after that it was like believing in Santa Claus

—though I mustn't scoff too much about that.

Too many of my contemporaries still believe.

A wind of some strength blew through the fields

moving the tall grass in all directions.

But in the forest all movement was frozen, and I was frightened.

Tonight I was tired, so very, very tired.

Through the day I had climbed into a dozen lawn trees

and then finally, with the help of a thirty foot ladder,

had scaled the highest point of the old barn's roof.

I sat there for a long time

looking out at my friends in the troubled, flaming forest.

Sometime tomorrow I would visit again and confront the situation,

but this night I was too tired and fell instantly fast asleep.

I dreamed of you, again, and loved you again.

But then for the first time you were sobbing

and I didn't like the dream any more.

"Please don't," I said, "please don't cry, I love you."

I was wide awake and very alert. It was six-thirty.

I knew the sun was beginning his climb over the horizon!

I knew, too, that the sobs and moans were not yours.

They were much louder now and came from deep in the forest.

Rushing to the window I looked out in that direction

and was amazed to see the trees moving in cadenced anguish.

I ran naked down the stairs, and out across the lawn and bean fields.

I heard the phone ringing. Was it you? I hope so. I love you.

I had raced to a point very near the creek and was still running.

My feet were torn and bleeding,

but I had to get to the near bank where the creek splits in two.

I had to get to the place where all of the big meetings were held.

I was almost there, when suddenly I was filled with wonder and awe.

My naked body was dripping raindrops

and wet leaves were matted on my forehead and face.

Yet I knew there had been no storms in the East for two weeks.

Even now the sky was blue and the sun was warming.

I stopped running, I had reached the meeting's epicenter.

The forest of love was weeping and now I knew—

The forest could laugh and cry and its tears were real, real tears.

"What's wrong," I asked, "please, please tell me!"

The forest was sobbing now. "Haven't you heard," it said,

"Haven't you heard of the happening?"

"The happening?" I said. "No, no, I have not. Tell me, please."

Our leader, it said, and the trees swayed left or right to look.

I looked too, and there before me only scant yards away,

lying on its side was the leader,

a giant and beautiful old maple tree.

"He died this morning," the forest said,

"and he never once complained."

Their tears covered my trembling body:

an eerie moan swept through the swaying trees.

"I'm sorry," I said, "I'm sorry.

Have you chosen another leader?"

The moaning stopped.

A gentle breeze signaled the forest to attention.

"We wondered," it said, "we wondered if you . . ."

Me," I said, "but how? I'm not even a tree."

The breeze blew again and falling leaves covered my entire body.

"No one will know," it said, "no one!"

"Now you are one of us."

"I can't" I said, "I can't" and tried to move away.

My naked feet were rooted and my long arms

reached toward the sun.

"Dear Sun," I said, "my young saplings cry for rain. Will you help us?"

The sun was smiling: a dark cloud appeared and covered his face.

The rain was gentle and warm,

and my forest was no longer weeping.

The End. . .

Except for . . .

Sometimes children walk through the forest

pulling at my branches, my arms.

They don't know of course — how could they—

that I am the leader.

They'd probably laugh at that anyway.

Why should trees have a leader. That's for human beings.

———

Many years have gone by now and the saplings,

those who cried for rain, are full grown and happy.

Often the young trees look up at me and ask my age.

I can't answer that; I can't because I don't remember.

I know what they're thinking—when will the happening happen?

Soon, but this time everything is ready for the new leader.

He has been chosen unanimously and with much love.

He walks amongst us frequently, always in deep meditation.

Occasionally he smiles through giant tears

and wild flowers reach up to him joyously.

Sometimes, when the snow falls, I think of something far away,

Something white. I can't remember more, I'm too old now.

Words come back to me from somewhere. But where?

I love you. And I love you too. Strange. What does it mean?